Transforming Small Business Sales with Social Media

Table of Contents

Your culture is your brand

Chapter 1. Introduction

Welcome to our Special Report: "Transforming Small Business Sales with Social Media"! This is the ultimate guide for those who aim to propel their small businesses to unprecedented heights! It isn't about complex algorithms, analytical tools, or daunting technical concepts – it's about the power of connections, the art of reaching the right audience, and transforming 'likes' into sales. Brace yourself for a comprehensive roadmap that's as enlightening and entertaining as scrolling through your favorite social feed, as we demystify the secrets of leveraging social media for business growth. Get ready to embrace those enjoyable 'aha' moments that turn small businesses into big players. Trust us, by the end of this exploration, you'll want to ditch the traditional approach and be ready to conquer the digital world! Get set, and embark on this thrilling journey with us!

Chapter 2. Understanding Social Media – Beyond Just 'Likes' and 'Shares'

Let's commence our exploration by addressing the central pivot of our discussion – social media. But what exactly does this term encompass? Most people imagine platforms filled with selfies, food pictures, and cat videos - a seemingly superficial world where the objective is to acquire as many 'likes' and 'shares' as possible. However, there's far more to it! Social media, in its modern construct, is a dynamic ecosystem of interactions, expressions, opinions, ideas, and much more. It's a place where brand stories are told, user experiences shared, and sales leads captured.

2.1. The Evolution of Social Media

Do you remember the times when social media was just a platform where people connected, chatted, and shared casual banter? Well, its capabilities have significantly evolved. Now, it's a marketplace, a news portal, a branding tool, a customer service platform, among other functionalities. With over 3.6 billion global users in 2020, it's a behemoth that commands attention.

Rewinding back to its inception, social media started as a tool to connect with friends and family. Think MySpace, Friendster, or the much-loved MSN Messenger. Then came Facebook, Instagram, Twitter, LinkedIn, Pinterest, Snapchat, TikTok, to name a few. These platforms not only kept the ethos of connection intact but also infused a commercial angle - a space for businesses to flourish. Transactions moved beyond conventional brick and mortar stores to virtual platforms, bringing in unprecedented dimensions of scale and reach.

To put it in perspective, about 71% of consumers are more likely to make a purchase based on social media referrals, according to HubSpot. Consider this scenario - You see a beautiful dress on a social media influencer's page; you like it, you 'like' it, and then you buy it. It's that streamlined!

2.2. Understanding the Influence of 'Likes' and 'Shares'

While it's tempting to synonymize social media success with the number of 'likes' and 'shares', it's precisely where most businesses get it wrong. The 'like' button is a powerful tool, no doubt. It gives an instant validation of the appeal and reach of a post. However, harvesting 'likes' is just skimming the surface of social media potential.

As a business, you should instead aim to create meaningful engagements and provide value, leading to longer and deeper customer relationships. These platforms can be effectively leveraged to build trust, ignite conversations, cascade messages, and influence buying behaviors. The 'share' button, when judiciously used, can make content viral, creating spirals of brand exposure.

2.3. Of User Engagement and Customer Retention

An engaging social media platform is like a bustling marketplace. Everyone's talking, discussing, joking, arguing – it's a hub of activity. It's where you, as a small business, can showcase what's unique about your offerings and why customers should choose you over competitors.

Effective engagement techniques include contests, quizzes, live videos, Q&A sessions, webinars, user-generated content, and influencer collaborations. Also, integrating feedback mechanisms and promptly addressing customer concerns improves service quality, satisfaction, and overall user experience.

The beauty lies not just in acquiring customers, but also in retaining them. A customer who feels valued, heard, and satisfied is more likely to return. Social media enables this personal touch, transforming customers into loyal followers and brand ambassadors.

2.4. Demystifying Sales through Social Media

Conclusively, we can't ignore that the ultimate motivation driving most businesses online is sales - a visible and quantitative metric of success. Social media can be an immensely powerful sales tool if used with strategic precision.

However, the sales process here isn't one-dimensional. It's a carefully crafted journey of brand awareness, understanding, consideration, decision, and then the purchase. This journey covers all touchpoints like social media ads, sponsored content, direct messages, comments, and product reviews. It's supported by characteristics like availability, convenience, personalization, and prompt service that social media enables.

To summarize, think of social media as an open canvas, ready to be painted with your unique brand story. Go beyond 'likes' and 'shares' - create value, build relationships, engage effectively, retain smartly, and sell creatively. Just remember, your small business is not small; it's compact, full of potential, waiting to unfurl its wings in the beautiful landscape of social media.

Chapter 3. Identifying the Right Platforms for Your Small Business

The first step of your transcendent journey into social media mastery involves understanding the diverse landscape of online platforms and identifying where your small business can thrive. Social media isn't a one-size-fits-all solution; different platforms have different uses, varying demographics, and unique business opportunities. Hence, selecting the right platform for your business is an amalgamation of understanding your business's needs, your customers, and the platform's capabilities.

3.1. The Overview of Major Platforms

Let us embark on a voyage through the wide landscape of major social media platforms and explore each one's features and differentiators.

3.1.1. Facebook: The Social Media Giant

With over 2.8 billion monthly active users, Facebook is undeniably the reigning king of social media platforms. It boasts a diverse demographic, making it an ideal platform for any business. What's truly special about Facebook is the combination of functionalities it offers: personal profiles, business pages, targeted advertising, groups, events, and a marketplace.

Businesses can create pages where they can post information, offers, updates, etc. Facebook Groups can also be an excellent tool for fostering discussions, loyalty, and a sense of community among your customers. Facebook's ad manager is a powerful tool, enabling targeted advertising based on user data.

3.1.2. Instagram: The Visual Powerhouse

Instagram shines through its emphasis on visual content – images and videos. It's the go-to platform for businesses that rely heavily on visuals like fashion, food, arts, travel, and lifestyle brands. What's more, it offers features like Stories, IGTV for longer video content, Shopping features for businesses, and targeted ads. Instagram's user base tends to lean younger, making it a good choice for businesses whose target demographic lies in the 18-34 age range.

3.1.3. Twitter: The Real-Time Network

Twitter thrives as a real-time platform. It provides an optimal environment for businesses to engage in ongoing conversations with their audience, respond to queries, or get involved with trending topics. Additionally, the platform allows you to 'tweet' brief updates, links, or other information to your followers, and it's an excellent tool for customer service and audience interaction.

3.1.4. LinkedIn: The Professional Network

LinkedIn is the platform for B2B businesses, professionals, and job seekers. It promotes networking opportunities, targeted advertising, and a space to share long-form content. Utilize LinkedIn to establish thought leadership, connect with potential clients, and recruit talent.

3.1.5. Pinterest: The Creative Catalogue

Pinterest's focus on discoveries, ideas, and inspiration broadens its reach to a variety of industries from fashion to interior design to recipes. Businesses can 'pin' images and organize them on different boards to showcase their products creatively, inspiring users to try new things or make purchases.

3.2. Choose Wisely: Matching Your Business with the Right Platform

Before jumping onto a social media platform, ask yourself these crucial questions:

1. Where is your target audience active?

2. Where is your target audience most receptive and engaging?

3. Does your product or service suit the platform's format?

Let's understand this with an example. If you run a digital marketing consultancy, your target audience - professionals and businesses - would likely be active on LinkedIn. It's on this platform that they'd probably be more receptive to your consultancy service offerings, given LinkedIn's professional context.

3.3. Engaging and Expanding with Multiple Platforms

Once you identify the primary platform for your small business, that doesn't mean you should forsake all others. Leveraging multiple platforms can be a game-changer for your brand and sales. It broadens the reach, drives more website traffic, and allows different content types to be utilized.

To leverage multiple platforms effectively: 1. Understand the content style and audience of each platform. 2. Create unique content for each instead of making duplicate posts across the board. 3. Keep the tone and messaging consistent across all your social media presence.

Always remember that the right platform can catalyze your small business's growth, paving the way for your ultimate triumph in the social media world. Identifying it requires rigorous research, understanding your business and audience, and strategic considerations. And once you find the right fit, harness its full potential to propel your small business sales to unprecedented trajectories. Embrace this journey and let the alchemy of social media transform your small business into a big league contender!

Chapter 4. Building an Effective Social Media Strategy

Beneath the veneer of the spontaneous and effortless aura presented by successful social media profiles lies an effective social media strategy. If you've been relying on instinct alone, this may be your awakening call. No matter how intuitive or creative you may be, strategy should be the bedrock of all your social media actions. We hope to ensure that the decisions you make — from posts to comments to likes to retweets — are strategic and intentional. Not a single action on any platform should be accidental or unthought.

4.1. Decoding the Meaning of a Social Media Strategy

To understand what an effective social media strategy is, we first need to deconstruct the term. A strategy is essentially a plan that outlines your business's goals and the steps you need to take, chronicling how you will achieve these aims. Merge this with social media, which is a tool to engage and communicate with a wide array of individuals, and you have a system that directs how a company presents its brand, connects with customers and achieves its sales objectives through social media platforms.

4.2. The Importance of a Social Media Strategy

The particulars of a social media creed differ for each business, replicating its uniqueness, values, and ambition. Still, all strategies share the purpose of outlining the plan for the future, setting definitive directions about what to do and how to do it. An effective social media strategy guides your actions and helps you gauge whether you're succeeding or sliding off track.

But why is a social media strategy important for your small business? Firstly, it helps identify your target audience and understand not just who they are, but what they value, where they spend time online, and what type of content they cherish. This knowledge is the cornerstone of any social media strategy, as your efforts would be futile if you're sending your message into a void, or worse, towards those who are immune to it.

Secondly, a social media strategy helps to define goals and objectives and align them with your overall business goals. It structures your efforts, creating a coherent narrative that your followers can understand and engage with.

Finally, a well-executed social media strategy promotes consistency across all platforms, maintaining your business' voice and brand, while also building a reputation and fostering trust with your audience.

4.3. Elements of an Effective Social Media Strategy

Now that you understand the magnitude of a social media strategy let's delve into the key elements that construct it:

1. **Set attainable goals**: This involves defining what you want to achieve from your social media efforts. Do you want to increase brand awareness? Drive sales? Improve customer service? Your goals will guide your strategy and help you measure success.

2. **Identify your audience**: Knowing who your audience is, is crucial for targeting the right individuals. This involves understanding your customer demographics, behaviors, and

preferences.

3. **Select your platforms wisely**: You need to be where your audience is. Carefully choosing the platforms that will best reach your target audience will enhance your ability to interact and engage with them.

4. **Analyze your competitors**: Understanding what competitors are doing can provide valuable insights. Analysis can help reveal opportunities, best practices, and areas that you can improve upon.

5. **Create and share valuable content**: Content is king in social media. It is the vehicle that delivers your message, and so, it should be enticing, engaging, and relevant. It must tell your brand's story and resonate with your audience.

6. **Engage with your audience**: The beauty of social media lies in its ability to allow businesses to connect with their customers in real-time. Engaging with your audience strengthens customer relationships and builds brand loyalty.

7. **Monitor and adapt**: Even the best strategies need tweaking. Keep an eye on your metrics, analyze your results, and adjust your strategy as necessary. In the fast-paced world of social media, evolution is key.

No one ever said it was going to be a walk in the park. But with the correct direction and a solid strategy in hand, navigating through the labyrinth of social media can be made simpler. It might take some time and patience to fine-tune your social media strategy but remember, Rome wasn't built in a day. With persistence and consistent efforts, you can cultivate an active online presence that builds customer relationships, enhances brand loyalty and, yes, even boosts sales.

Chapter 5. Creating Engaging Content: 'The Art of Storytelling'

The realm of social media is a storytelling hotbed that, when properly harnessed, can be a game-changer for small businesses. As master storytellers, we can lure the audience into our created universe, making them see, feel, and ultimately, believe in our unique offering. Keeping that in mind, let's delve deeper into the art of storytelling and how it can be thoughtfully integrated into your business's social media strategy.

5.1. The Essence of Storytelling in Social Media

In contemporary marketing, storytelling serves as a cultural adhesive, binding together businesses and customers around common values, aspirations, and experiences. It's no longer about bombarding your target audience with dry statistics or sterile sales pitches. Instead, it's about selectively crafting narratives that emotionally resonate with your audience, compelling them to interact, engage, and ultimately convert.

Small businesses, with their close-knit customer base and distinct local flavor, are in a unique position to weave emotive and character-driven narratives that can make strong, lasting perceptions. The cherry on the frosting? Stories are inherently social, making them tailor-made for social media environments where sharing, interacting, and engaging is the order of the day.

5.2. A Six-Step Approach to Stellar Social Media Storytelling

Let's break down the process of creating engaging story-driven content for your social media channels into six comprehensive steps, each tailored to optimize your storytelling strategy.

1. **Identify Your Unique Narrative:** Every small business is a story in perpetual motion. Start by identifying the unique aspects of your business - the origins, the victories, the challenges, and most importantly, the people. These will form the backbone of your storytelling strategy.

2. **Understand Your Audience:** A successful story is one that echoes with its listeners. Understand the aspirations, challenges, values, and preferences of your audience. Craft stories that speak their language, address their concerns, and resonate with their ethos.

3. **Define Your Story Arc:** A compelling story follows a logical structure, with a clear beginning (setup), middle (confrontation) and end (resolution). This provides your audience with a complete experience, which in the context of business translates to problem-identification, solution-presentation and a clear call-to-action.

4. **Choose the Right Social Media Platform:** Different platforms cater to different audiences and content types. Choose your platform based on your target demographics and the nature of your story. Instagram is ideal for visual stories, while Twitter is excellent for quick, impactful narratives, LinkedIn is perfect for professional and business-oriented tales, and Facebook provides a mix of all.

5. **Use Engaging, Authentic Content:** Be it high-quality images, immersive videos, captivating text, or interactive polls, ensure that your content is authentic, appealing, and in sync with your

brand identity.

6. **Don't Sell, But Inspire:** The purpose of storytelling is not solely to sell, but to inspire, to connect, and to build relationships. Direct selling may repel customers; instead, subtly weave your products or services into the narrative and let them discover the value for themselves.

5.3. Unleashing the Power of User-Generated Content

User-generated content (UGC) is the real-world manifestation of the ancient practice of communal storytelling, marking a shift from brand-centric to consumer-centric narratives. UGC, which includes customer testimonials, reviews, unboxing videos, and usage experiences shared online, provides authenticity and credibility to your brand like no other form of content.

To tap into UGC, encourage your customers to share their experiences with your product or service. Craft campaigns that incentivize customer engagements. Remember, each shared experience is a story that can boost your brand's credibility and desirability.

5.4. Leveraging Storytelling Tools on Social Media Platforms

The beauty of social media storytelling is that each platform comes with its own unique set of storytelling tools.

Instagram, for instance, offers 'Stories', 'Reels', and 'IGTV' for longer narratives. Instagram's 'Shop' feature also allows seamless product tagging within stories, blending your narrative seamlessly with direct selling.

Facebook 'Stories' follow a similar model, with additional features like the 'Instant Experiences' for immersive, mobile-optimized storytelling. Twitter, apart from its crisp textual narratives, also offers 'Twitter Moments' for curating multiple tweets into a single story.

Each tool offers a unique way to communicate your story. Hence, it's essential to understand their potential and adapt your content accordingly.

Storytelling on social media is a potent tool for small businesses. Its strength lies in its ability to humanize brands, to strike emotive chords, and to create contagious narratives that boost visibility and engagement. By mastering this art, you can transcend the product-centric paradigm to create an immersive brand universe, building not just customers but brand advocates in the process. Remember, in a world that's increasingly selling, people are longing for entities that are sincerely telling. Be that breath of fresh narrative air, and watch your small business rewrite its growth saga!

Chapter 6. Power of Visuals: Leveraging Images and Videos for Higher Engagement

In a world where everyone is glued to their screens, the sway of visual content is impossible to deny. Images, infographics, and videos have established their reign over text-based content, emerging as highly effective tools for demonstrating products, communicating brand stories, and sparking emotional responses.

6.1. The Impact of Visual Content

Today, it's imperative for businesses to understand the power of visuals. Oftentimes, consumers make decisions based on first impressions, which are usually driven by visuals. Be it images, videos, or infographics, visual content is easier to comprehend and remember than dense blocks of text. It key reasons for this lie in how our brains process information: visual data is processed 60,000 times faster than text, and around 90% of the information transmitted to the brain is visual.

Consider a scene wherein a potential customer is scrolling through their social media feed: will they be more likely to stop for an intimidating chunk of text, or a visually appealing post? The latter almost always wins. Captivating visuals generate user interest and engagement, increasing the likelihood of your content being shared and spread to a wider audience. This amplifies your brand's visibility and reach, creating room for increased sales.

6.2. Adding Images: Worth a Thousand Words

Images can articulate complexities in a way that textual content often fails to achieve, showcasing products and services in a more tangible way. Show your business offerings in action, or exhibit the end results of using them. Before-and-after pictures, product demonstrations, tutorials, and customer testimonials in picture format not only provide insights into your offerings, but can also build users' trust in them.

Images also have the advantageous feature of being consumable. With most online audiences skimming rather than reading in-depth, an informative image can provide a lot of value in a small amount of time. Additionally, original graphics, like infographics or data visualizations, can offer a unique way to disseminate often tedious information.

6.3. The Rise and Dominance of Video Content

Video content holds a unique place in the field of social media, providing an interactive, dynamic and immersive way of engaging with an audience. It immediately catches a viewer's attention and keeps them entertained, all while communicating important messages about your brand or product. From demos and reviews, through testimonials, to behind-the-scenes peeks, videos enable you to not only sell your product, but also sell the experience that comes with it – what some call 'the power of the show, don't tell.'

Social media platforms have adapted to this trend by excitingly evolving their video capabilities. Consider Facebook's auto-playing videos and 360° videos, Instagram's IGTV, and TikTok's branded challenges. The sheer variety of video formats allows for a lot of experimentation and engagement with different platform features.

6.4. Engaging through Live Streaming and Stories

Live streaming and Stories are innovative visual content features on social media platforms, and offers a more immediate and authentic way to connect with your audience. By offering insights into the behind-the-scenes aspects of your business, you are humanizing your brand and creating a stronger bond with your audience. Use these real-time, disappearing posts to host Q&As, demonstrate product usage, announce new products, or showcase corporate culture.

6.5. Working with Visuals Effectively

To tap into the power of visuals, four crucial aspects need to be considered: relevance, quality, consistency, and accessibility. It's crucial to ensure that your visual content mirrors your brand's identity and resonates with your target audience. High-quality images and videos are an absolute must; otherwise, the message you're trying to get across might get lost in pixelation. Consistency in style, tone, and color scheme will aid in brand recognition and loyalty, while adding alt-texts and descriptions help your content remain accessible to users with visual impairments, ultimately benefiting all users by enhancing your SEO scores.

6.6. Tracking Performance and Taking Action

The beauty of social media is that it provides tools to measure the impact of your visual content. Key metrics such as likes, shares, comments, and view durations help track user engagement levels. Social media platforms also provide valuable insights like demographics, best performance time, and more. You should use these metrics to understand your audience better and optimize future content strategies.

To sum up, visuals are a powerful asset for businesses in this era of social media, enabling them to hold the attention of increasingly distracted audiences, evoke emotion, and convey complex concepts clearly and instantly. By investing in compelling visual content, small businesses can level the playing field with their bigger counterparts, carving out their space in the bustling social media world, and boosting their sales in the process.

Chapter 7. Building Relationships: The Key to Social Selling

Whether you are an artisan peddling unique crafts, a small-scale restaurant ensuring your community has a taste of the world, or a tech start-up that dreams of breaking the market mould, relationship building is as essential as the value you provide through your product or service. Such relationships are what breed loyalty and ultimately, sustain long-term growth.

7.1. Establishing Genuine Relationships

A dynamic universe in itself, the sphere of social media possesses the uncanny power to influence, inform, inspire and, most importantly – connect. Unlike outbound marketing techniques – which have a more direct, 'hard sell' approach – social media selling focuses on building relationships. But what does this mean?

In the realm of social selling, true relationship-building transcends beyond the passive act of gaining followers or likes. It revolves around creating a two-way stream of conversation, offering value beyond your product or service, and establishing yourself as a 'friend' in the eyes of your consumers. This social friendship, in turn, births brand affinity and trust, which are precursors to frequent purchases and word-of-mouth recommendations.

7.2. The Power of Connection

When connection turns into relationships, that's when your social media campaign truly takes off. It's not just about the metrics anymore; it's about engaged followers who look forward to your posts, interact with you, and come to see your brand as more than just another business. It's about fostering a community, not cultivating a customer base.

The real metric to look out for here is engagement. It's these comments, shares, and Direct Messages (DMs) that paves the path towards fostering a durable relationship. We recommend not just responding to these messages swiftly, but also personalizing these interactions. After all, who doesn't appreciate a customized, human-like interaction, as opposed to automated, monotonous replies?

7.3. The Art of Social Listening

Yet, building relationships isn't confined to the parameters of mere responses. It reaches out to the often overlooked, yet powerful tool of 'Social Listening'. This implies monitoring your customers' needs, complaints and viewpoints, even if they aren't directly communicating with you. It's about combing through the myriad posts of the digital world and looking for mentions of your brand, related keywords, competitors, or anything relevant to your industry.

By employing social listening, you delve into the minds of your customers, coming face-to-face with their likes, dislikes, aspirations, and needs. This understanding, combined with empathy, equips you with the power to serve at a higher level, ultimately multiplying your chance of securing a sale.

7.4. Personalizing Your Approach

Personalization is a tool that has to be wielded with finesse for it can often make, or break, your relationships with your followers. More than just addressing your followers by their names, personalization spans understanding their interests, recognizing their challenges, and addressing their pain points with your product or service.

In this context, platforms like Twitter and Instagram can be gold mines of information. Their open-ended nature of conversations and the power of hashtags can give you a peek into your customers' lives. This insight goes a long way in creating a bond built on understanding and mutual value addition.

7.5. Collaborative Engagement

Engagement and interaction with your followers is another aspect of relationship building. This includes liking and commenting on their posts, sharing user-generated content, and inviting them to be part of your journey. You could organize contests, Q&A sessions, polls, or requests for feedback. This collaborative engagement nourishes the relationship by making your follower base feel valued and heard.

7.6. Transforming Chats Into Sales

The key to successful social selling is to avoid overtly selling. Remember, the primary goal is to forge strong relationships that can naturally lead to sales, not to push your products or services aggressively. This philosophy lets you focus on generating valuable conversations in your comment sections or DMs, turning your social media platform into a bustling marketplace teeming with life – a marketplace where bonds are formed, and brand loyalty is created.

7.7. Conclusion

In the digital age, where the line between real-world contacts and virtual connections is progressively becoming blurred, prioritizing the art of relationship building is more critical than ever. Whether you believe it or not, each 'digital handshake' can be as impactful, and potentially more far-reaching, than a physical one. So set foot on this trail, delve deeper into your social media platforms, connect with your audience, and catapult your small business to a big-league player. Social selling isn't about algorithms or fancy lingo - it's about relationships. So gear yourself, roll up your sleeves and plunge into the exhilarating world of social selling. The wind of success is in your sails.

Chapter 8. Utilizing Paid Advertising: When and Why?

In the world of social media marketing for small businesses, engaging content and organic reach play an undeniably vital role. They allow you to foster relationships with your audience, build a loyal customer base, and shape your brand's identity in the digital world. However, there's a gear in the online marketing machine that can supercharge your efforts: Paid Advertising.

Considering this, one might wonder, "Why would I pay for advertisements when I can reach my audience organically?" This question is understandable, but it discards the fact that organic reach has its limitations. It seldom guarantees that your content reaches the right people at the right time. It fails to ensure that your meticulously crafted postings get the spotlight they deserve in the fast-paced, crowded social media landscape. This is where the magic of paid advertising comes in.

8.1. Understanding the "Paid" in Paid Advertising

To comprehend why and when you should resort to paid advertising, it's crucial to get a grasp of what it entails. Paid advertising is a type of social media strategy that involves promoting your brand or posts through sponsored advertising. This essentially means you 'buy' a privilege: Your content gets a front-row seat to your chosen target audience, regardless of whether they follow your business or not.

Unlike organic reach, paid advertising provides you with an opportunity to display your content more prominently. This allows your brand to reach audiences that have a high potential of converting into loyal customers. What's more, with this strategy, you get access to robust targeting features that can focus on specific user demographics, behaviors, and interests.

8.2. Weighing the Need: When to Choose Paid Advertising

Paid advertising is not a one-size-fits-all solution. That said, knowing when it is an optimal strategy for your business largely depends on your marketing goals. Below are circumstances when paid advertising should be under serious consideration:

1. **Achieving Quick Results**: When your business targets short-term goals like launching a new product, kick-starting a promotion, or gaining quick visibility, paid advertising can offer instant exposure.

2. **Enhancing Brand Awareness**: Paid advertising allows you to attract and engage an audience beyond your organic reach, boosting visibility, and hence, brand awareness.

3. **Driving Website Traffic**: When you aim to increase your site's visitation rates, paid social can help direct traffic to your digital doorstep with specific call-to-actions.

4. **Promoting Content**: If you have high-quality content that just isn't making its way through the noise, sponsored ads can ensure it gets the attention it deserves.

5. **Targeting A Specific Audience**: If you're looking to tap into a particular demographic, location, or group based on interests, paid forms allow you to better refine your target, ensuring your content reaches the right people.

8.3. Delving Deeper: Why Use Paid Advertising

Understanding when to use paid advertising is only half the game. The other half involves recognizing its benefits and why your small business would benefit from it.

Maximized Visibility: Paid advertising ensures your content doesn't get lost in your audience's crowded feed. It gives your brand a prominent presence, increasing the likelihood that your message is seen and heard.

Targeting Capabilities: Paid social platforms come with sophisticated targeting features. You can target content to people based on demographics, location, interests, behavior, and even based on their connection to your brand or followers.

Budget Control: You have control over how much you want to spend on your ad campaigns. Whether your budget is large or small, you can leverage paid advertising to get the most value.

Robust Analytics: Paid advertising platforms offer in-depth analytics to measure the performance of your ads. This data provides critical insights to optimize ads, improve return on investment (ROI), and meet marketing goals.

Control Over Ad Placement: Not only do you get to select your target audience, but you can also choose where your ads will appear, be it on Instagram stories, Facebook news feeds, or LinkedIn's professional timeline.

8.4. Using Paid Advertising Wisely

While paid advertising has many benefits, utilizing it efficiently requires a strategic approach. It's not about pouring all your resources into this channel but rather understanding where it fits into your overall social media strategy.

Investing in understanding your audience, defining clear goals and key performance indicators (KPIs), testing different ad variants, regularly reviewing and tweaking your campaigns based on performance analytics, are all integral to an effective paid advertising strategy.

In summary, striking a harmonious balance between organic social media efforts and paid advertising is not only recommended but essential to maximizing your online presence. Done right, this synergy can be the tool propelling your small business to new heights of success and beyond.

Chapter 9. The Secret Sauce: Influencer Marketing and Collaborations

In recent years, influencer marketing has emerged as a dynamic and profitable marketing strategy. It banks on the power and reach of popular personalities on social media platforms who have an established following – known as influencers. Social media collaborations, on the other hand, involve partnering with other businesses or brands in a mutually beneficial arrangement. Both these strategies entail an effective combination of trust, authenticity, and brand affinity, which profoundly impact a brand's performance and outreach.

9.1. Embracing Influencer Marketing

Influencer marketing is all about promoting your product or service through individuals who have a significant influence on people's purchase decisions. These influencers often have a large, dedicated following on social media. The concept is based on trust; followers admire their influencers and trust their recommendations. This trust and relationship is what small businesses can leverage.

To integrate influencer marketing into your sales strategy effectively, consider the scale and relevance of the influencer. Choose someone whose lifestyle aligns with your brand and has a following that consists of your target audience. Ensure you're not merely blinded by the massive following; the influencer's followers should be people who would genuinely be interested in your product.

Once you've found the right influencer, the content they create should vary – product or service recommendations, tutorials, reviews, unboxing experiences, or regular posts with your product integrated subtly into their lifestyle. The essence lies in weaving your product or service seamlessly into the influencer's narrative, making it feel organic rather than forced.

9.2. Exploring Collaborative Opportunities

Collaboration within social media marketing can significantly boost your brand's visibility, outreach, and engagement levels. By leveraging the strengths and followers of other businesses or individuals who align with your ethos, you can create unique and engaging content that appeals to a broader audience.

Contacting potential collaborator candidates should always be done professionally, with a clear understanding of what both parties stand to gain from such a partnership. Consider collaborations such as shared live videos, co-written blogs, cross-promotion of each other's products, giveaways, and joint webinars or workshops.

Remember, the key is to find businesses or influencers that complement your brand, rather than compete with it. Sharing mutual benefits is critical, be it in the form of audience sharing, information exchange, or content creation.

9.3. The Do's and Don'ts

While influencer marketing and collaborations can be extremely lucrative, they come with their challenges that need to be navigated smartly. Here are some points to keep in mind:

- **Do** take time to vet any potential influencers or partners. Check their online presence, engagement rates, type of followers, and past partnerships.

- **Do** establish clear expectations and agreements. Transparency in terms of payment, content creation, timelines, and deliverables helps in successful collaboration.

- **Don't** go for influencers or collaborators solely based on follower numbers. Consider the quality and engagement level of the followers.

- **Don't** force a product or a message. Keeping promotions authentic and inadvertent is crucial for acceptance amongst followers.

9.4. Evaluating the Success

Just like any other marketing effort, the success of the influencer marketing and collaborations needs to be measured to justify the time, effort, and money invested. Key metrics to monitor should include engagement rates (likes, comments, shares), follower growth, web traffic originating from the influencer's platform or collaborator's page, and increase in sales.

In sum, influencer marketing and collaborations are potent tools that can be very effective for small business sales strategy, when applied with discernment. They can provide brands with credibility, awareness, increased traffic, and ultimately, higher sales. Small businesses should tailor these strategies to their needs, industry specifics, and target audiences. In doing so, they may find the secret sauce for their unique growth recipe in today's digital marketing landscape. Whipping up this mixture of influential figures, symbiotic collaborations, and authentic engagement can lead small businesses to experience flavors of success they might have otherwise overlooked.

Chapter 10. Tracking Success: Key Performance Indicators and Analytics

In the complex world of social media marketing, it's essential to have a firm grasp on how well your strategies are performing. To turn aimless posts and haphazard picture uploads into meaningful, successful marketing, it's vital to wade into the world of Key Performance Indicators (KPIs) and analytics.

10.1. Navigating The World of Social Media KPIs

KPIs are data-based metrics used to measure the effectiveness of various business operations. When applied to social media marketing, KPIs track specific goals and objectives, revealing whether your campaign is successful or, if it's falling flat, providing insights into areas for improvement.

For instance, let's consider a basic KPI – the number of followers or 'Likes' your business page has. This may seem a simple vanity metric, but it's a profound indicator of your brand's reach and popularity among internet users.

10.2. Diving Deeper: Advanced KPIs for Social Media

To get a deeper understanding of audience engagement, marketers delve into a myriad of advanced KPIs such as reach, impressions, engagement rate, clicks, shares, comments, video views, and more.

'Reach' measures the number of unique users who viewed your post, while 'Impressions' account for the total number of times your content was displayed, regardless of whether it was interacted with or not.

'Engagement rate' gauges the scale of interaction with your content. It assesses the total sum of likes, shares, and comments divided by the total impressions or reach (depending upon your preferred method), times 100, giving you a percentage rate of engagement.

'Clicks' are a surefire way to understand content appeal and generate leads, as they show the number of times users clicked on a post or ad, leading them to your landing pages or websites.

Each KPI serves a distinct purpose and, when tracked diligently and analyzed correctly, can unlock untapped potential for your small business.

10.3. Harnessing the Power of Analytics

Next, we step into the technicolor sphere of analytics. While the term may seem daunting, at its heart, analytics simply aids us in understanding the underlying patterns in our data.

Social media platforms come equipped with built-in analytics tools. Facebook has its 'Insights', Instagram offers 'Instagram Analytics', and so on. These tools churn raw data collected from your social media operations and deliver it in digestible bites of information – from demographic data of your audience to which posts have the highest levels of engagement. Harnessing this data is the key to crafting successful campaigns.

10.4. Utilizing Analytics to Inform Strategy

Armed with the powerful knowledge gleaned from your KPIs and analytics, it's time to put it to work to amplify your sales. Use the insights to reveal what works (and what doesn't) for your audience. Based on data, modify your social media business strategy and tailor it to inculcate more of what the audience loves.

Say, for example, you notice a spike in engagement on Tuesdays. Then, that's when you should go all-in and post your critical content. Similarly, if videos get more engagement than images, it's a clear call to action for you to invest in more video-based content.

10.5. Rising Above The Data: Making Informed Decisions

While the advantages of proficiency in KPIs and analytics are enormous, it's also easy to get lost in the overwhelming sea of data. Therefore, it's key to stay focused on the metrics most relevant to your business goals and to use these metrics to inform your decisions.

And remember, success seldom lies in pursuing every metric that comes your way but lies instead in identifying what is truly relevant to achieving your objectives.

By deploying KPIs and analytics painstakingly and wisely, a small business owner can not only transform their social media presence but also turn 'likes' and 'shares' into tangible sales, bridging the gap between cyberspace and the real world, and between your business and unprecedented success.

The path toward mastering KPIs and analytics isn't always easy, but it is certainly worth it. After all, a small pivot, guided by well-informed data, can make a world of difference to your business progress. Just remember, the data doesn't lie – let it guide you to your brand's true path of success.

Chapter 11. Future of Small Business Sales: Keeping up with Social Media Trends

Engaging in a dance with the whirlwind of social media trends can either be an exciting adventure or a daunting ordeal, depending on how well-versed you are with the ever-changing landscape of digital spaces. Failure to adapt, however, is not an option for businesses yearning for growth. The art of succeeding in this realm is rooted in an ongoing learning process that never ends.

11.1. The Importance of Staying Current

The main reason why keeping up with social media trends is essential for small businesses lies in the intense competition and the constant evolution of customer preferences. Social media is more than just a platform for sharing cat videos, memes, or aesthetic photos; it has become a crucial meeting point for businesses and customers. As platforms evolve, so do the ways in which consumers interact with brands and express their needs and desires. What may have been a brilliant strategy a year ago may no longer hold relevance today, as customer behaviors undergo perennial shifts.

In a digitally-savvy world, people are no longer merely passive consumers of marketing messages. They actively participate in curating their online experiences, seeking value, authenticity, personalization, and convenience, among others. Therefore, businesses have to look for trends that will allow them to meet their customers' expectations continuously. Falling behind on these trends may isolate the business, rendering it irrelevant and out of touch with its customer base.

For instance, consider the relatively recent booming popularity of short-video content, like TikTok or Stories on Instagram and Facebook. Agile companies promptly incorporated these features into their social media strategies. However, others that kept clinging to older formats, like long video content or text-heavy posts, lost potential opportunities to engage a broader audience in tune with these trends. Small businesses simply cannot afford to overlook these shifts in consumer preferences.

11.2. Identifying and Adapting to Social Media Trends

Given its dynamic and evolving nature, keeping up with social media trends can seem overwhelmingly complex. However, the process can be simplified and streamlined by practicing a few key steps.

Conduct Regular Social Listening and Monitoring

Through social listening, companies can identify new trends by watching for shifts in conversation topics, hashtags, shares, and other activities within their market. Monitoring tools, like Hootsuite or Brandwatch, can help track and analyze these changes, providing valuable insights into the evolving preferences and behaviors of their audience.

Analyze Competitor Activities

Keeping a close watch on successful competitors is another effective way to stay updated on the latest trends. A detailed examination of their content, tone, engagement strategies, and audience feedback can orbit you towards current and potentially beneficial trends.

Attend Webinars and Online Training Programs

Participating in webinars and online training programs hosted by social media experts can be an excellent source of comprehensive and up-to-date information about current trends. In addition, these programs usually provide valuable insights and tips on implementing new strategies.

Utilize A/B Testing

Experimentation is the heart of digital stability. When a new trend emerges, don't just jump into it unprepared. Instead, run small A/B tests to gauge its effectiveness before you decide on a full roll-out. This way, you can guard against potential risks while seizing opportunities.

11.3. Trends to Watch Out For in the Near Future

To give you a head start, here are some of today's most promising social media trends that you might want to consider exploring:

Live Streams and Video Content

With people spending more time online due to the pandemic, live streams and video content have seen a massive upsurge in popularity and are likely to continue riding the wave in the foreseeable future.

Artificial Intelligence and Chatbots

AI-powered customer service, like chatbots, is revolutionizing the way businesses interact with their customers. They are efficient, save time, and enable the delivery of personalized service round the clock.

Stories and Disappearing Content

A great hit among millennials and Gen Z users, Stories on Instagram, Facebook, and LinkedIn, and disappearing content on Snapchat, are leading the trend towards temporary, easy-to-digest content.

User-Generated Content

UGC creates a sense of community around a brand and is perceived as more authentic than traditional advertising. It's an effective way to gain trust, create engagement, and powerfully market your products and services without overt selling.

In conclusion, staying updated with social media trends is not an option but a necessity to ensure future small business sales. Depending on their ability to adapt, the digital world can either become a gold mine of opportunities for small businesses or a maze with no visible exits. Embracing change and fostering a flexible mindset is consequently critical to stay relevant and sustain growth. Remember, digital marketing is all about creating experiences and interactions, and the more efficient you are in achieving this, the more successful your small business will be in this digital era.